Rosy Carrick is a writer and performer based in Hebden Bridge. She has a PhD on the poetry of Vladimir Mayakovsky and has released two collections of his work in translation: *Volodya: Selected Works of Vladimir Mayakovsky* (Enitharmon, 2015) and *Vladimir Ilyich Lenin* (Smokestack, 2017).

Rosy's theatre debut *Passionate Machine* won the Best New Play award at Brighton Fringe and the Infallibles Award for Theatrical Excellence at Edinburgh Fringe in 2018, before touring internationally throughout 2019. Her critically acclaimed second play *Musclebound* premiered in 2022, and toured from 2024 to 2025.

Rosy's debut poetry collection *Chokey* was published by Burning Eye in 2018.

I LOVE

ROSY CARRICK

Burning Eye

BurningEyeBooks
Never Knowingly Mainstream

Copyright © 2025 Rosy Carrick

The author asserts the moral right under the Copyright, Designs and Patents Act 1988 to be identified as the author of this work.

All rights reserved. No part of this publication may be reproduced, stored in a retrieval system, or transmitted, in any form or by any means without the prior written consent of the author, nor be otherwise circulated in any form of binding or cover other than that in which it is published and without a similar condition being imposed on the subsequent purchaser.

This edition published by Burning Eye Books 2025

www.burningeye.co.uk

@burningeyebooks

Burning Eye Books
15 West Hill, Portishead, BS20 6LG

ISBN 978-1-913958-52-7

For Olive Bee Carrick
I love you most of all

'Since it was to end so soon, I almost wish I had never heard it. For it has roused a longing in me that is pain, and nothing seems worth while but just to hear that sound once more and go on listening to it forever.'

Kenneth Grahame, *The Wind in the Willows*

Contents

Animal Etiquette	11
I Love	13
Birthday	25
Major	27
Ladybower	29
Autophobia	32
Lost Boys	35
Piggy in the Attic	37
Twiglets	38
Fridged	39
Winner Takes All	41
O, live!	43
About That	45
Cavendish	50
Souvenir	51
Hydrant	53
Timo	56
Mayday	61
Imaginary Advice	63
Poem	65

Animal Etiquette

The lot
of the crucified child,
grown up,
is to be the human equivalent
of those canine heroes
from the start of time,
compelled
by animal etiquette
to remove their bottoms
on entering an establishment
and to hang them on hooks
as we might hang up our hats
until, one fateful night
at the all-dog
annual banquet,
an electrical fire broke out
and, in the frantic scrum
for smoking bottoms,
each dog grabbed what it could
without looking:
long and short hairs jumbled,
tails limp,
anuses cramping –
but every throat barking:
the wrong thing is better than no thing at all.

It is easy,
in our present day,
to pour scorn
on the hybrid fruit of their loins,
yanked outside by the neck
every morning
to piss and shit –
all power having,
since their ancestors' days of glory,

been leeched
by homo sapiens invaders
for whom one tragic night
that was nobody's fault
had never dictated
a lifetime's distracted yapping
after every potential
back-end match
they meet:
could this one be mine?

                               or this one?

       or this?

But what the dog has
that the invader does not
is the community
of its fellow mongrels
who see its privation,
who feel as it feels
and who know
what it means to survive.

I Love

1.

In my friends' eyes,
there is a virus
eating my heart alive,
and so
for my sake,
they tell me,
they've
decided to starve it of oxygen.

In reality,
the virus
eating me alive
is in my own eyes
and, thriving on darkness,
every time I blink,
my blood-retinal barrier
shrinks my capacity
to see
when a symptom
presenting as one thing
is really another.

Intellectually,
I know
there is a human being
                           out there,
                                    somewhere,
                                                  alive –
in the literal sense, at least –
and doing its small best
to be unutterably dull,
but then the telephone goes
and I love

electrocution torture
for how it makes
even the weakest back
bridge
until the muscles
                explode; for how
it makes them
          slacken
                  to water
only after
      the burnt entreaty
                        MAKEITSTOP
gets stuck
      in the throat of its victim

as much as the next dehydratee
holding herself
             up
               by the neck
from the drinking trough
                        decade after decade
so as not to degrade her appetite
for peace

but, even so,
torn connective tissue takes time to repair
and
I need to know
where my agency ends
and involuntary contractions
make me
mechanical.

2.

Nobody doubts
that
infra-ultra-radiation
skirts the edges of human perception
but nevertheless exists—
I throw back
in the face of my diary,
whenever this virus
eating me alive
in my own eyes
splits you
        into
            the visible light
                      of your spectrum

and provides no mnemonic
to organise
your rainbow of

- the tempered pane, sealed inside its window frame against freedom
- the gurning tongue with no allocated colostrum
- the storm surge, indifferently stripping its corpses
- the cost of lamb neck
- and the destitute kiss

that does not render
'and of this place,' thought she, 'I might have been mistress'
corrupt and ridiculous,
even to me.

3.

You
keep me awake at night
and I can't stand it.

        snell
I   that
                   line
                       to
                         the
                         shank
                      of
                    my
                  hook
            to
         tension
      a
    culprit
  to
 thrash
against
when
I'm ovulating
and in the mood
to rejoice in the fact
that the ribbon
caught on the fence
might not delude itself
with the thought
that it is dancing –
or that it
and the splinter that pierces it
are anything other than an accident
of friction –
but that I am more optimistic
than ribbon,
whose humiliating task is limited

to trimming,
tying,
binding the delicate skin of its object,
forever *out*side where I stay
in,
wristbone-deep, fisting
the joy out of everything;
when reality shares its doughnut with *me*,
I insist on the hole
and make *it* keep hold of the ring!

4.

A love that never grows
                            stale
is not to be sniffed at;
there is no risk
that, surfeiting,
the appetite may sicken and so die
if, when the body aches
                            to be held,
its love is always elsewhere,
                                 declaring
itself through radio waves
like the syllable alone
is filling enough to
get fucked by,
though
all the lonely body really craves
is to be fought for
                            by something
prepared
          to press naked
against its belly:
something heavy
to fall asleep to
                    in
                          that petrifying stretch
                                          of dark
when the ceiling's bare spots melt
into an almost-readable threat,
and the pulverised heart
needs a partner to steady its beat to.

5.

I know everything
there is to know
from overhearing
a sobbing woman
explain to her friend on the night bus
how her collie bitch had died:

her husband
had noticed the collie bitch had a tick
that wouldn't let go
so he had held her down
and twisted it;
and when that didn't work
his friend had held her down instead
so the husband could attack that tick with a scalpel
and put an end to his bitch's screaming,
but the plasmic tick he held in his hand
triumphant at the end
was a nipple,
and the bitch bled out.

6.

Intellectually,
I know that,
when I do not stop to think,
I feel
I love;

and,
when I stop to think,
I fear
I only need;

and long
have I tried
to demarcate the healthy
from the rotten,
but

it's not possible
to deblue
a block of Stilton,
and you and I
have also cultured
too much all-one-body
to undo.

Intellectually,
I know
that that's not true;

I know

that love is not a boat;
it's glue,

and I am stuck to it, not you;

and just as,
if
 a tongue
            attacks
                        a salt lick
                                    wrapped in plastic,
it will not get through,
so
   being stuck to love
means love –
like Lucky Pierre –
by touching both,
divides us both
in two.

7.

When you miss your cue
or get your lines wrong in the dialogue
I've scripted and telepathised,
a small and hungry part of me
complains
that it's not possible
to keep this virus closer
than a wife, closer
than an eye,
and to keep myself
at the same time
sane;

and even when I counter it
by switching my allegiance
to the ethos
of the
        factory
        fur farm
        operative,
baffled and amused
by the *mindless* behaviour
of the caged mink
gnawing its own legs off,
thinking only of gore
damage
done to the product,
it persists.

At times like this,
I am vulnerable
to the influence
of my ignorant friends,

who take my stammering affect
to mean
        that the Eloi
                had been right all along;
whose attempts
to invalidate my
double slit experiment
by crushing what
I know is right –

that the plate
retains its status as a plate
whether or not it is piled with food;
the evacuated fat cell shrinks
but is a fat cell still
and may or may not be refuelled;
but the void,
if filled,
is, by definition,
no longer a void –

must be,
at all costs,
avoided.

8.

I love myself
best
by locking the door
and carrying about
my forearm
like a baby
        that has grazed its knee:
gazing down at it,
cradling its back
and mopping up the blood.

The baby is too young
to know
that
    the phototactic reflex of a moth
is no different from that of a sunflower,
but that,
       unlike the flower,
the moth has not got the luxury of soil
to stop it
compulsively
flipping its back
             to the limerent object
it takes to be moonlight
and spiralling;

the baby is too young
to be afraid
of staying up late
to observe love's potential
collapsing
from wave into particle
on the detector screen
that this virus,
eating me alive
in my own eyes,
refuses
to keep financing.

Birthday

Sorry to disturb you
while you're sitting with your friends
have lovely hair –
it's my daughter's birthday tomorrow
my daughter is coming
to stay at my house
is so much colder in the summer
than the winter it seems
strange.

I've put twenty pounds
in the birthday card
has a twenty-pound note
paperclipped inside
the card
is for grown ups
so she must be older than a child
can be so difficult
to raise on your own are you
okay?

I've looked and looked
for a piece of paper
to wrap her present
you see
is a T-shirt from that shop I like in the centre
of Norwich is heaving again
and again but I just can't seem to find any.

The night before my seventh birthday
I was so excited I couldn't sleep.
I invited my whole class to my party
and in the morning watched thirty jellies
set in bowls.
I wore a stripy outfit;

it looked like a dress
but was really a shirt tucked into a skirt.
There were so many prizes
and, except for Claire Rathburn's stupid brother,
everybody loved me.

But I think I may have told you that
I'm waiting in for the call
I got from my grown-up daughter
this morning
might have been the call I was
waiting for a call
can be so frustrating.

I think pink paper should be fine
if she's a girl
after all
she's not here yet,
is she
here already?

A gift bag would be perfect, thank you,
I'd love to sit down,
I've hurt my toe,
I don't know how
I got into
your garden
is beautiful
things always make me feel a little bit sad
sometimes.

Major

My unanswered texts
                        pile up
                                on each other's
                                                weak backs
all night
like geeks
        breaking into a party,
and I see you
            have seen me
                        for what
I am: nothing
            but fear
                    at a pitch you don't want
to hear sing.

As usual,

I have said too much too soon.
I was too wide open.
Too easily some
                thing
                        to use.
I poured myself out so quickly
I spilt,
and,
    across your impossible torso,
the champagne bubbles I'd advertised
became screwworms
rooting for any way in.

I mean, who,
I picture you
demanding of the mirror,
once I'd finally fucked
off,

your eyebrows twisted
                        like an autism card
                                          for revulsion,

worth keeping,
would force so much
of something so precious
onto someone so new?

IDST: I fawned
and worshipped myself
out of existence
until,
invisible,
I crawled by your feet,
making slippers of my fingers,
declaring my love
like a sunburnt baby declares its splitting skin.

In bed,
we breathed the same breath
back and forth
between our hot sealed mouths
until the edges went black
and, steamed wide open,
all my pain fell away.

And I forgot,
               in the euphoric bliss,
                              my lot: I am
as foster is to adopt; I am
as Friday's cocktail is
to Monday morning's clocking-in card.
Facts
       are facts
               aren't personal. Some
kittens get kept; some suffocate. It's just that
that is that.
Please stay. Your ardour
pushed bacteria into my bladder through my urethra,
and today the price is mine alone to pay.

Ladybower

My mum
gives me
a bin bag
to fill
with things
to get rid of
and I try
to get away
with not losing
nearly everything
I love
but she sees
my stone
in the shape of a pig
and says:
it is not worth keeping.

My eyes
want to stay
a long time
staring
at the picked-off
wood chip
pockmarks
over my headboard
but I am too busy
to play,
patting
the yellow flank
of my skirting
to thank it
for all of its company.

And when the water comes,
I cry
and my mum says:
it's only bricks
and mortar;
we can start again now,
we can be a bit richer –
but what about
if
when
the weather is hot
the gateposts
poke up
and everyone sees
my bedroom
undrowned

or my
best doll,
Baby Darling, left
inside the toilet
with the lid down
and her hair
cut off on
the last day
to punish her
for never fighting back
and for never telling
whose big feet
ought not nightly
to have loved butter
but did?
I don't know

how long
suffocated plastic
takes to break
down;
I don't know
how
to get back
and check
from the new house;
I don't know
how low
the level needs to be
before
everyone will see
what I did
except me.

Autophobia

I've always wondered:
what tips a person over
into thinking an all-beige outfit
is a great idea?

It doesn't matter
how keen a gardener
you were in your youth;
premature fruit drop will terrorise you
as much as it does your neighbour.
They'll tell you it's pests and diseases,
adverse weather
and herbicide drift,
but the reality is:
a flower, once bloomed,
cannot stay soft forever.

At what point
does an animal,
anyhow,
turn into meat?
When it dies?
When it gets sealed
into its plastic packet?
Or when it's still jammed
in its shit-smeared confinement crate,
dreaming of a buttermilk bath?

I used to get so wet
over those emails
we would send each other,
but recently I rooted them out
and they're so misogynistic –
I was ashamed of myself
and astounded
at your poor gynaecological knowledge.

Old people have started
saying *hello!*
as they pass me by on the street.
They think I'm one of them,
I suppose;
my £1.50 Oxfam coat
does look like something Nora might wear
in *Last of the Summer Wine.*

Do you remember
that horrible cesspit
where the queuing men
all secretly took their condoms off
and turned me into a gloryhole
while you got sucked off
by the sixty-eight-year-old paunch
with a mouth like a nostril?
I'm not sure I'd want to go back there again,
but then
one bad penny doth not a bad purse make

and, deep in my oestrus,
I can't stop fantasising
about tight sequined dresses
and discos –
licking the glitter
off strangers' cheekbones –
sweating my MDMA out
and shouting *lipsalve for all!*
as I plunge a hundred hot fingers
into my cocoa butter tin.

But that was then
and this is Norwich,
and, scrolling the government death toll
as I unpack my weekly vegetable box
and make plans
to live

with a man
I do not love,
it is impossible
to pretend with you
that none of this is happening,
or that I am still in Brighton
and alive.

My greatest fear
is that one day,
rather than automatically chucking
the turnip and swede
in the compost bin,
I'll cook them into a wholesome stew
and say,
Gosh, how simply delicious!

Lost Boys

You might be able to force your arm
through the plastic to the pink part
of the chocolate, if you
roll up your sleeves,
two familiar boys explained,
drumming on the kitchen table.

My feet were on fire
and the bucket of water,
painted in stripes with a starling,
was outside,
but there was no need to worry:
my pain was only a 3.5,
according to the chart
their dad had glued onto the fridge
in July
to stop them from getting confused.

But have you been getting my letters?
I asked them,
turning a bloated red pepper
from the fruit bowl
around in my hands,
its seeping flesh
too much for the leathery skin;
and they faltered, suddenly
less keen to show me
the figures they each had got
for Christmas,
and told me they'd received two
back in the summer,
if that's what I meant?

I pictured envelopes
kissed into letterboxes
month after month, ripped
into the bin by hands
that now stroke the face
of their replacement mother's
replacement.

I was afraid of this,
I told them.
I have dreamt about it often;
even this exchange is a dream!
And, in slow motion,
they nodded
their acknowledgement,
solemnly shook their heads,
their hair so soft and well cared for,
and dribbled
back into the floorboards.

Piggy in the Attic

Piggy in the attic   Piggy in the attic
Piggy in the attic   Piggy in the attic
Piggy in the attic   Piggy in the attic
Piggy in the attic   Piggy in the attic

Piggy in the attic   Piggy in the attic
Piggy in the attic   Piggy in the attic
Piggy in the attic   Piggy in the attic
Piggy in the attic   Piggy in the attic

Piggy in the attic   Piggy in the attic
Piggy in the attic   Piggy in the attic
Piggy in the attic   Piggy in the attic
Piggy in the attic   Piggy in the attic

Piggy in the attic   Piggy in the attic
Piggy in the attic   Piggy in the attic
Piggy in the attic   Piggy in the attic
Piggy in the attic   Piggy in the attic

Piggy in the attic   Piggy in the attic
Piggy in the attic   Piggy in the attic
Piggy in the attic   Piggy in the attic
Piggy in the attic   Piggy in the attic

Twiglets

Toni had the Chopper
she'd got for her birthday,
so Anna and I took the rejects:
riding, one-handed
to the sewage works gates
at dusk
on the last day
of summer.

We called up our red-hot
leather-clad boyfriends
on pieces of twig
to explain
that, although
our mums had gone
and grounded us
for smoking,
we couldn't wait to kiss them
on Monday. Then,

keeping our lips sealed
tight against the danger,
we took it in turns to burst
through gathering swarm
clouds of midges,
pumping our fists
like we'd just smashed
through that huge paper barrier
marked with a G
and come first
in the final of *Gladiators*.

Fridged

I don't always see myself
wrapped in plastic,
pulled from a river;
sometimes I squirm
on the boss's lap
and laugh at the office party;
sometimes I lose my grip
on the kitchen knife
on parquet tiles. There

is usually someone
following me home,
though each time I jump
it's only a jogger
or cats
fighting over a carcass.
And yet,
just my luck:
whether I am a barrister,
a babysitter,
a nightshift waitress
squeezing the cash
in my denim jacket pocket,
the second
I let my guard down
– bam –
the hessian sack slips over my head
and the van door
slams. Often it seems

I am happiest being a housewife,
except there is always a strange man
creeping around in my home
while my husband is working late
or has broken down

on that receptionless road
as his meatloaf gets cold
on the table again. Somehow,

he has learnt how to stay safe:
though slight in build,
faced with an assailant,
his punches land
hard, while I,
somewhere miles away,
spin brittle as the plastic doll,
as a child,
I loved to wind up in my jewellery box,
watching
my throat skilfully slit
from behind
in the bathroom mirror.

There's an art to surviving your woman.
Right now, he'll be screaming fists
through doors,
tossing off his Ray-Bans
to identify remains
found
in the scrubland
I so adored
to walk our healthy sons in,
flexing his jaw till the muscle pops
as detectives list off buffer men
they think may be responsible

and nailing all his extra lines
while I,
as all my sex does best,
sit scriptless at the makeup mirror,
dreaming of a leading role
and washing rope burn off my wrists.

Winner Takes All

Awarding every belligerent gamer
millions of fans
and fitting spikes to buildings
deters Britons –
normally a sentimental bunch –
from plunging off a harbour wall
when the first costly bite of a pasty
on a beautiful ride to work,
filled with music
and the proximity of the masses,
threatens the embattled
imposter.

When it comes to starvation,
it is futile
to fight back
against entertainment.
Pamela,
a holidaymaker,
explains the reason why:
the herring gull cannot afford
a night out
violence-free
and will,
no matter that
chips come cooked,
don its tunica molesta.

Thus, blighted
and besieged,
the pavement shares its horror stories:
technology is whetting
the rich's fingers;
beady eyes saunter down
the slot machines
in coastal settlements –
rubbish in the streets –

in July
a girl will be airlifted to hospital;
blood will pour down
her ice cream,
her arms distributing delight
while statistics point
at the brightly coloured bunting
of abandoned shoes
and silence
rewards our sacrifice.

O, live!

I haven't forgotten
that Wednesday night,
when we peaked too soon on purpose
and you told me
you felt like your job had been
only to keep me alive
in my vulnerable youth
and that,
now I was fine,
you didn't know
what you were here for.

I am sorry
for how openly and often
I must have told you
loving you
had taught me how to love
myself and how to want to live.

The day I waved you
off from home
for the final time
and the train doors clicked,
blood sprang,
unscheduled,
out of my womb
and I couldn't
bring myself
to bin the ruined pants;
the most painful part
of being a mother
is knowing success
will one day
render you
obsolete
and I have never felt

more flimsy
or afraid of the dark
than in those first years –
irrefutably on my own
at last –
when I thought
no longer having a daughter
to buy flat peaches for
meant never eating
flat peaches again.

It was you
who taught me otherwise –
remember that.
You have no job
except to let your name
become the anagram
I love.

About That

I know you think it's something suspicious
still to be breaking the skin
as a woman
the age I am;
the maladroit need to summon my blood,
to know I have something in here
to bring to heel.

You used to cut
pictures
of Elizabeth Hurley
out of the Saturday TV guide
and stick them into a scrapbook,
but then you grew up,
got married,
put your inheritance down on a mortgage,

cheated on your wife
with hundreds of women
while she stayed home
with your children,
and finally left her
for me,

so I do understand why
balancing over my pan
of boiling water
makes you need to feel certain
the rod of your life
is a fork,
not a piece of spaghetti.

You know nothing about physics
but you hate it
when your sausages burst
so you prick them all over to fry them;

likewise,
baking potatoes get stabbed;
it's what you do
to stop
hot things exploding.

They used to incise birthing women too:
a Glasgow smile for the mouth
of every vagina
to hurry things up
and protect against
unpredictable female tearing,

but an arbitrary scalpel in the wrong hands
and the husband stitch
caused damage
bodies like yours have zero context for,
and too little interest in fixing,
so they stopped it.
There is a difference,

in your opinion,
between the ice pack you press
against the muscles
of your post-hike back
to numb the pain
and my technique
of counter-irritation,
and yet,
when you say my strategy
upsets you,
in return
I do not say:
I don't
expect
you
to
understand
the grammar of a language

you never had to learn
existed,
but please try,
you ignorant fuck,
and comprehend that
while you've been waxing
your quiff in the mirror,
singing along to your own shit songs
and dipping your toe
in the shallowest end of my intellect,
I have been struggling
to allow
a flooded lung
that has no throat
to breathe,
and it is expensive

to have one's
– if imperfect,
if precarious,
nevertheless – best
and most efficient
lifeboat
consistently mistaken for a shark
and harpooned.

Of course
I would like to live on dry land
and sunbathe
with you
explaining
again
how Brian Eno's brother's dog
is a huge fan of your oeuvre,
but I can't survive
at the same time
in two places
and something is stuck

in the field
where I was walking:
she is seven,
like me,
but not like me
she is forced to lie on her back
because her legs have been cut off
at the hip
by the man who is raping her torso.
He will kill her next,

but it is important
to separate
the music
from the man,
say all the men
in the meeting rooms that,
as an adult,
it is my portion
to inhabit,
and nothing I argue
will stop you belauding
the *genius*
of his anti-establishment
noisescape
as you book him in
as the headline act
of your festival.

I would not be caught dead
in your company
sharing that sentence
out loud;
I would not permit,
even, the noxious
intellection to form.
To think,
I thought
that thought was involuntary

action once:
a sort of
        oozing
                secretion of the brain,
and not the lifelong gluing up
of a broken lock.
It's not my fault

if I'm like crack
to public schoolboys
making up for what they lack
in life experience
with confidence,
though I must confess
I, too, fetishise
the irresistible way that
rigid buttery soldiers like you,
sheathed
in the gold
of my finite yolk,
make everything look so easy.
I understand now

why you refuse to buy
your butchered meat on-bone:
it is the worst thing ever
to cling to a lover
with whom you are so intimate,
and to feel so terribly lonely.

Cavendish

Are you okay, darling?
I love you.
That makes two of us.
Anna works too hard.
Get her to slow down,
for my sake.
I love her,
tell her.
Is she drinking?
Does she drink milk?
I can't remember.
Get her to drink milk.
Lots of milk.
How long do you think I've got?
Water.
Have you heard from Ned?
Water.
Please help me.
Okay, darling.
Make everything colder.
Icy water.
I don't want to sit up;
I want to lie up.
I'm not surprised,
Bee is so clever.
Help me.
Get me out of here –
get me out of here now.
Water.
Water.
Water.

Souvenir

Do you remember that time
you broke into my house
and, without saying a word,
you laid three Polaroid photographs down
on the green leather panel
of the desk I got for my birthday
when I was eighteen?

Rocking back and forth
on your feet
like first-prize cava
ready to blow,
you wanted me to know
you had toyed with a man,
rubbing your thumbs
across the rim of your belt,
and I couldn't put my finger on the smell.

The first shot was bleached out,
taken too close:
two men too busy laughing
to pay attention
as they draped rope
around the chest
of their victim:
a tracksuited Laocoön,
his eyeballs grappling the ceiling in horror,
attacked by his sons,
throttled by serpents,
protected by no one.

Next, the same men
posed around a table,
the two on either side
modelling axes while

the third sagged between them,
seated, his forehead low,
his arms taped down horizontal
at the wrist and the elbow.

The third image was
a confusion of vomit
and ash-green skin.
The gormless hands had been
awkwardly repositioned
alongside the forearms,
and the seated man –
like a novice magician –
had been reminded to smile for his audience.

Do you remember how
I just sat there,
gluing my stare to those
white pimpled strips you get
on the base of instant prints,
and keeping my cool?

I had forgotten that rock
that squats in the belly,
picturing Olive
asleep in her bedroom,
dreaming of Winnie-the-Pooh.

And how,
before you left,
you touched me on the shoulder?
You wanted me to know
that the man you had seen that night
was still alive;
that you had put his lumps of meat
in a freezer bag,
offered to call the police on his behalf –
and that he had declined.

Hydrant

It's embarrassing
when someone offers
my youngest child
a book
of matches
to light her cigarette
and I lose my shit;

when,
showing off,
she goes to kill a tealight
with her fingertips
and I slap her hand
and spit on the wick.
It makes her cringe;

I don't want her
to grow up
afraid to order a meal
in case
it comes served
on a chafing dish,

so, privately,
I do try
to teach myself
a lesson:
I stare into the August sun;
I stay in a boiling bath too long;
I sing out loud
that 'London's Burning' song
until the syllables feel alien –

but I just can't seem
to stop
my muscles
jumping the gun
when they think
they've heard
the lost two letters
of the word
I won't let back
into my house:

The first is in elephant but not in stair.
The second is in star but not in twinkle.
The third is in [———] but not in winkle.
The fourth is

When I was twenty-two,
I watched my eldest child get burned alive:
she was pinned under something that would not yield
in the living room
when something caught alight
and I didn't know how to act.

I watched
as the carpet skinned her knees;
I watched
as she almost split her spine to release herself
but I knew all the while
that you can't win a fight with nature,
so I just stood there –
and my child watched
straight back,
distracted
as though
behind my eyes
a video played
and the actor's name
was right on the tip of her tongue;

not able to grasp,
in the moment,
the meaning
of her melting scream
or why I,
of all people,
did not take up the fight
where she was failing.

In one hymnbook
of my memory,
I tried;
but in the torn-up rest
I know
I only breathed in smoke
and suffocated
in the place
I could not see
her sacrum any longer.

The moon,
eclipsed,
appears
to perish wholesale in the sky,
but it comes back
in time.

I wish someone had said that,
once.
I watched the lights go dull;
what kind
of mother
lets the same thing
happen twice?

Timo

Ever since I first met you,
I have been the victim
of intrusive thoughts
that if I were
illegally
to sublet my flat on Airbnb,
the incoming party
might not only bury you
in a mountain of salt
but do it while drinking wine
and laughing
and filming it all on their mobiles.

The suprachiasmatic nucleus
is an extraordinary feature:
even cortical circuits
kept in a petri dish
can tell the time,
but, like anything alive,
they are easy to manipulate.
Did you know
there are laboratories
in which
simple everyday torches
are employed on timers
to convince cells to divide
at what they think is night
and multiply –
against the natural reflex
of their true circadian rhythm?
The duped cells do replicate
but the daughters they make
are smaller,
weaker,
and condemned
to be short-lived.

That night I saw your lung pore
for the very first time
ought to have been ecstatic,
but all I could think was:
what if one day
a horrible child
pokes a match into that –
and should I do it myself,
to short-circuit my itching
and finally get some sleep?
In theory,
I do have that power, but,
pathetic as I am,
even in my loneliest moments
I would get up in the night
and disturb your trajectory
from the fridge to the oven
and back to the fridge
to choke you
with a wooden stick
no sooner than I'd gnaw through
my father's throat
for the pleasure of eating an apple.

Buy a glass tank and trap it,
say my well-meaning family and friends,
as though I had not a gazillion times explained
that the elementary grains that make up our world
are not contained in space
but that they themselves create that space;
they interact incessantly;
they exist only
through their incessant interactions,
and this reciprocal interaction is,
in itself,
what we call
the happening of the world.

That Australian teen
who died
from eating a slug
on a dare
is repugnant to me,
and not just because
I would kill to discover
the trace of your trail in my butter
right now
but, in terror
of what it might mean if I did,
I, instead,
as usual,
do the sensible thing
and book myself into a twelve-bed mixed-sex dorm room
so I can stay up all night
and listen to people breathing,

but
because,
in this life,
some things are simply right
and some are wrong.
It is not okay,
however much one wants one's friends to admire one,
to transfer to oneself
a condition
caused by the parasitic worm
found either in rodents
or those who eat rodent excrement
and to cause such pain to one's family,
year after year,
while one lies drooling in a coma,
merely because,
for one,
certain lives are worth expending
on a whim.

People say
when we focus
obsessively
over an object of love
we're really running away
from something we fear
in ourselves –
but then 'people'
like the film *La La Land*
and buy bacon for 99p;
even the notoriously black
'black holes'
are not actually black:
they glow like a hot body,
and the smaller they are,
the harder still they glow.

Whenever I am asked
to swallow a secret
that sets my gullet on fire,
and am instructed
to keep my mouth shut
while I am eating,
I can lie like a corpse
on the kitchen floor
and wait there for you to find me.
One night, my scotopia
transformed you
into an almost-decapitated mouse,
your whiskers quivering,
trapped by something unseen;
occasionally,
you turn on your heel and curl back on yourself
in a way I didn't even know was possible,
looking so bewitchingly like a glistening turd
on the vinyl;

but mostly,
our mutual respect
and independence
mean that I don't see you at all,
and then I wonder
if I have taken what I read online
about gastropods
being capable of love
too literally.

It can be frightening
in the pitch black,
when my overworked rod cells
can't quite get a grip
on my outline
in the bathroom mirror
is too distorted
to know if my eyes are even open
or not – do you feel that too? –
how the embodied soul
greyly flickers
its unblurred granularity
and fears
what it feels:
that *'I'* am too small;
some *'me'* keeps breaking through uncheckable?

Mayday

I dreamt
        I was
                a piece
                        of fish
                                that never got
to sleep
        on white plates
                        it had never seen
                                      my edges
flaking up
        in grief

I set
      three bells
                  to ring
                        each day
                              to wake
to send
        me back
                to bed
I scribbled
          worries
                  from my head
                              in pencil
till the page
          was grey

the third
        bell
              pregnant
                      as a seed
                                will never sound

was never set
    is there
        to make sure
            I forget
                I've lost
something
    I think
        I need
           I dreamt
I was going
    to kill
        my child
            I was going
to kill
   myself

I took
   the pillow
       from its shelf
            but
never
   reached us
       both
           in time

and I
   screamed
       like a mockingbird:
                To arms!
                To arms!
                To arms!
                To arms!

I called back meaning to alarm

and
   no one said
a word

Imaginary Advice

Did you ever listen back to that
episode where I was stuck to the
flocking of a double
inflatable mattress, adrift on a
manmade pond, surrounded by
realistic synthetic boulders
like you get in a zoo, but inside – like
The Crystal Maze – while
seven pre-programmed mechanical walruses
breached around me in
a synchronised figure-of-eight routine,
precisely designed to signal the
fact I was never allowed to escape?

If not,
you might not remember that the
pond was installed as the
central prop of a
medium-budget,
Arts Council funded,
live audience podcast recording – by a
writer famously allergic to kittens –
on the subject of
'ostranenie'; whose
most popular feature was the underground
Barton's vintage doll's house containing a
miniature model of
me, as a child, dressed in the
reproduction of an outfit I wore at a
party in 2022, alongside a
model of
famous scientist
Dr Emmett Brown completing some
paperwork, while,
on his real knees in the

doll's-house kitchen, a
naked, ballgagged, grown-up man –
painted in all the relevant places
to suggest muscularity
where, when you looked
more closely,
there was none –
spitroasted himself alive,
like a chicken, in
an oversized oven, with
an actual chicken dangling –
dead – on a
chain from the
flesh of his chest;

and even though,
officially,
there was no
audience participation allowed,
my favourite part was
when you squirted your milk from
underneath the lighting rig and
said, in response to the question
I did not ask, the
phrase I did not need to
understand
to get:
inviolable
except by death.

Poem

Sometimes I'm sad
but nobody knows,
and then the tears trickle
right down past my nose.
There's no one to talk to,
to tell how I feel;
they'd think that my sadness
was not at all real.
So I hug my best teddy
or play a good game
but a few minutes later,
I'm crying again.
I keep on trying not to weep
and eventually I fall asleep.

By Rosy Leaver

Acknowledgements

I am very grateful to my dear friend James Burt and my daughter Olive Carrick, both of whom have supported me without fail over the last five years (and beyond); I would be lost without you. I am also grateful to Keston Sutherland and Sam Turton for some very helpful and insightful editing suggestions, and to Ashley Clark for advising me on the cover design.

Thank you to everyone else (and, again, to everyone mentioned above) who has given me advice and feedback, engaged with – and provided space for – the development of my work, inspired me, driven me wild with desire, cooked for me, put a roof over my head, financially supported me, and generally looked after and loved me. I really appreciate your kindness and care:

Lucille and Maxine Allan, Hannah Ayin, Ros Barber, Toni Beardmore, Katie Bonna, David Bramwell, Polly Carrick, Edward Carrick-Leaver, Nathan Filer, Steve Forster, Kate Frances, Jenny Greenshields, Helen Gregory, Alice Helps, Cleria Humphries, Peter Hunter, Toria Garbutt, Peter Gray, Roni Guetta, Anna Jefferson, Anna Jepson, Sally Jenkinson, Helen Jewell, Marina Kobler, Robin Lawley, Debbie, Norman and Sam Leaver, Nick Lezard, Joe Luna, Anna Mathers, Jamie Martin, Hollie McNish, Jess Moriarty, Michael Parker, Chris Parkinson, Steph Potts, John Osborne, Rosie Phillips-Leaver, Kitty Peels, Jennifer Pittman-Cownie, Ashley, Benjamin and Eleanor Pittman, Rebekah Pledger, Lucie Regan, Iain Rodger, Sooxanne Rolfe, Anne Rupert, Jon Seagrave, Kate Shields, Beverley Scott, Kat Sinclair, Gilly Smith, Year Solver, Dan Spicer, Jake Spicer, Verity Spott, Lucy Turton, Nozomi Uematsu, Erika Jessica Walker, Rachel Weston, Lesley Wood, Naomi Wood and Juliette Wright.

Thank you additionally to Clive Birnie at Burning Eye for your wonderful support and enthusiasm for this collection, and to Harriet Evans for your keen editorial eye.

'Major' was shortlisted for the Cheshire Prize for Literature 2024/25.

Finally, in the UK as in many other countries, women are being harmed and our fundamental rights denied as the police and courts are failing to deliver justice after sexual violence. If you would like to support campaigns for a justice system that is fair and equal, and which provides better support for survivors, these organisations are a good place to start:
endviolenceagainstwomen.org.uk
centreforwomensjustice.org.uk

www.ingramcontent.com/pod-product-compliance
Lightning Source LLC
Chambersburg PA
CBHW022121090426
42743CB00008B/945